MARK
BATTERSON

THE

GOD

ANTHOLOGY

EXPLO
DEPTH   GOD

LifeWay
Biblical Solutions for Life

Published by LifeWay Press®
© 2013 Mark Batterson

ISBN: 978-1-4158-7580-3
Item: 005539340

Dewey Decimal Classification Number: 231
Subject Heading: GOD \ PROVIDENCE AND GOVERNMENT OF GOD \ THEOLOGY

Unless otherwise indicated, all Scripture quotations are taken from the
Holman Christian Standard Bible®, copyright © 1999, 2000, 2001, 2002
by Holman Bible Publishers. Used by permission. Scripture quotations
marked NIV are taken from the Holy Bible, New International Version,
copyright © 1973, 1978, 1984 by International Bible Society. Scripture
quotations marked ESV are taken from The Holy Bible, English Standard
Version® (ESV®), copyright © 2001 by Crossway Bibles, a publishing ministry
of Good News Publishers. Used by permission. All rights reserved. Scripture
quotations marked (NLT) are taken from the Holy Bible, New Living
Translation, copyright © 1996. Used by permission of Tyndale House
Publishers, Inc., Wheaton, IL 60189 USA. All rights reserved.

To purchase additional copies of this resource:
ORDER ONLINE at www.lifeway.com;
WRITE LifeWay Small Groups; One LifeWay Plaza; Nashville, TN 37234-0152;
FAX order to (615) 251-5933 or PHONE (800) 458-2772

Printed in the United States of America

Adult Ministry Publishing
LifeWay Church Resources
One LifeWay Plaza
Nashville, Tennessee 37234-0152

CONTENTS

ABOUT THE AUTHOR   4

INTRODUCTION   5

1   MYSTERY   6

2   HOLINESS   20

3   INCOMPARABILITY   36

4   MERCY   50

5   JEALOUSY   64

6   SOVEREIGNTY   80

LEADER GUIDE   96

ABOUT THE AUTHOR

Mark Batterson serves as lead pastor of National Community Church (*www.theaterchurch.com*) in Washington, DC. One church with seven locations, NCC is focused on reaching emerging generations. The vision of NCC is to meet in movie theaters at metro stops throughout the DC area. NCC also owns and operates the largest coffeehouse on Capitol Hill.

Mark has two Masters Degrees from Trinity Evangelical Divinity School in Chicago, Illinois. He is the author of numerous books including *In a Pit with a Lion on a Snowy Day, Wild Goose Chase, Primal: A Quest for the Lost Soul of Christianity, Soulprint* and *The Circle Maker*. Mark is married to Lora and they live on Capitol Hill with their three children: Parker, Summer, and Josiah.

You can follow Mark on Twitter at @markbatterson or check out his blog at *www.markbatterson.com*.

INTRODUCTION

There is nothing more important than a right understanding of God. Every day we have fears, concerns, and demands that distract our lives and compete for our attention. Before long, we begin to filter God's character and nature through our experiences, creating a god in our image. *The God Anthology* is about defining God based on … God … as He has revealed Himself to us in Scripture.

We pray that this study of God's character and nature stirs up in you a hunger for God and drives you deeper in His Word. We believe that you will find God far more wonderful and powerful and good and intimate than you ever dared dream. And in that place, we hope that you discover you are not less important than you thought but in humble confidence find your rightful place as heirs, sons and daughters in His kingdom.

Ultimately, the goal is that we would also enter into a deep and transformative repentance. Repentance calls us to leave. It requires that we turn 180 degrees and shift our focus from ourselves onto the Person and work of God.

We most commonly hear testimonies of what we have been saved *from*. We hope that our corporate testimony—full of little individual stories—will speak of a God whom we are called *to*, and the beauty of what life with Him is all about.

Finally, if you come away with only one thing from *The God Anthology*, let it be this: "He must become greater; I must become less" (John 3:30, NIV). May that be true in our own lives as well.

SESSION ONE

MYSTERY

God is never boring. Frustrating, perhaps. Confusing, enlightening, shocking, even funny. But never boring. If we think that God is boring, then we are obviously worshiping a God of our own making and not the Creator, Redeemer, and Sustainer of the universe and of our lives. Growing in my knowledge of and relationship with Christ is always an adventure. The more I learn about God, the more I realize how little I really know about Him.

God is incomprehensible, but the mystery of God is revealed in Christ. There are some things we will always wonder about and question because God's thoughts are higher than our thoughts, and His ways are higher than our ways.

One of the most dangerous tendencies we have is to deify man and humanize God. We give Him human characteristics and reduce Him to someone we can completely understand. In the beginning, man was made in the image of God, but we've been making God in our image ever since. We reduce the mysterious God down to the logical constraints of our left brain and, in that process, all the mystery is lost.

One of the first things we learn about God is that we just can't quite figure Him out. There is an element to His transcendent, omnipotent, omniscient character that remains a mystery to us. With God, dirt can become the medicine that heals and love can become the best weapon we can wield. In the mystery of God, we discover life in death and abundance in sacrifice.

Let's take God out from under our microscopes and analytical boxes and let Him display all of His power, majesty, and glory to us. When we revel in His mystery, worship happens, and life becomes much more exciting.

Use this time to talk as a group about …

What first comes to mind when you think about God? List two or three characteristics that you most associate with Him.

What are some of the characteristics of God that are most confusing, frightening, or unsettling to you?

If you could ask God any question, what would you ask?

What are some of the places in Scripture or moments in your life when God seemed most mysterious to you?

List two words you would use to describe yourself—words that define who you are now.

Fill in the blanks below on important points as you view the message from Mark. You'll unpack this information with the group after the video.

Our biggest problem is our _____.

The goal isn't just to know more information. The goal is _____.

One of our most dangerous tendencies is to _____ man

and _____ God.

If you lose the mystery, it is called _____.

Humility in the presence of mystery is called _____.

We offer answers; God offers a _____ through Jesus Christ.

JOB 11:7, NIV

Can you fathom the mysteries of God?

1 CORINTHIANS 2:9-10, NIV

"No eye has seen,

no ear has heard,

no mind has conceived

what God has prepared for those who love him." —

but God has revealed it to us by his Spirit.

The Spirit searches all things, even the deep things of God.

PSALM 46:10, NIV

Be still, and know that I am God.

1 CORINTHIANS 8:2, NIV

The man who thinks he knows something does not yet know as he ought to know.

- A low of view God is the cause of a hundred lesser evils and a high view of God is the solution to 10 thousand problems.

- There are more than 400 names for God in Scripture and each one reveals a different dimension of His personality.

- We want a Twitter God we can reduce to 140 characters; a God we can put in nice, neat categories; a God we can understand; a God we can measure; a God we can comprehend; even a God we can control. But God doesn't fit in 140 characters.

- God is mysterious. The more we know, the more we know how much we don't know. The more we know, the greater the mystery. And that should make us fall in love with Him even more!

Mark uses the watermelon seed and theological tension to illustrate the mystery of God. What are some other examples you see in creation that reveal and celebrate the great mystery of God's character? What are some of the apparent theological tensions that remind you that there is a mystery to be explored?

SMALL-GROUP DIALOGUE —

1 CORINTHIANS 2:1-10

When I came to you, brothers, announcing the testimony of God to you, I did not come with brilliance of speech or wisdom. For I didn't think it was a good idea to know anything among you except Jesus Christ and Him crucified. I came to you in weakness, in fear, and in much trembling. My speech and my proclamation were not with persuasive words of wisdom but with a powerful demonstration by the Spirit, so that your faith might not be based on men's wisdom but on God's power.

However, we do speak a wisdom among the mature, but not a wisdom of this age, or of the rulers of this age, who are coming to nothing. On the contrary, we speak God's hidden wisdom in a mystery, a wisdom God predestined before the ages for our glory. None of the rulers of this age knew this wisdom, for if they had known it, they would not have crucified the Lord of glory. But as it is written:

> *What eye did not see and ear did not hear,*

> *and what never entered the human mind—*

> *God prepared this for those who love Him.*

Now God has revealed these things to us by the Spirit, for the Spirit searches everything, even the depths of God.

Paul was a highly trained, educated, and skilled man. In other places in Scripture, we find him contending for the gospel against the brightest philosophical minds of Athens on the Areopagus, sharing the story of Christ with the political leaders of the Empire, and cleverly stirring up theological debates between members of the Sanhedrin. However, Paul recognized that there was a point at which he must come to the end of his brilliance and knowledge. In this letter to the church at Corinth, he admits that God cannot be contained by the hundred trillion synaptic connections that crisscross our cerebral cortex.

Paul contrasts human wisdom with the mystery of God. How should human wisdom be used?

Paul also speaks about the role of the Holy Spirit in helping us grasp the mysteries of God. Why do you think it is important to know that the Spirit "searches everything, even the depths of God"? What do you think this has to do with our relationship with God?

DEUTERONOMY 29:29

The hidden things belong to the LORD our God, but the revealed things belong to us and our children forever, so that we may follow all the words of this law.

I admit, I have a Deuteronomy 29:29 file. It's the place where I store the questions and circumstances for which there is no logical explanation. There are some things that will remain a mystery to us as long as we live within the space-time dimensions of earthly history.

What questions would you put in a Deuteronomy 29:29 file?

What life circumstances would you put in a Deuteronomy 29:29 file?

When God's actions don't seem to correspond with what you think you know of the character and promises of God, what do you do?

ROMANS 16:25-27

Now to Him who has power to strengthen you according to my gospel and the proclamation about Jesus Christ, according to the revelation of the mystery kept silent for long ages but now revealed and made known through the prophetic Scriptures, according to the command of the eternal God to advance the obedience of faith among all nations—to the only wise God, through Jesus Christ—to Him be the glory forever! Amen.

Romans is the closest thing we find to a systematic theology in the New Testament. In this letter to the church in Rome, Paul outlines in bold detail the content, implications, and application of his faith. He closes with this idea that ultimately, Jesus Christ is the mystery of God revealed.

What are some things we learn about God's character and ways through the Person of Jesus Christ?

In looking at the life of Christ, where do we see the mystery of God in full display? In other words, where do we see truth in the tension of opposites, the foolish confounding the wise, or unconventional approaches to faith and action?

How does it make you feel to know that there will always be certain dimensions of God's personality and ways that remain a mystery to us?

Paul closes out the Book of Romans on a note of worship. That's where good theology should always lead us. How does knowing that God is Mystery lead you to worship differently?

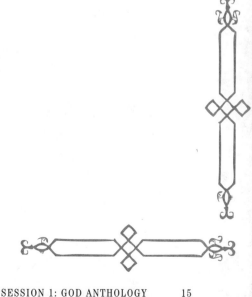

WRAP ─────────────────────────────

Ephesians 2:4-5 explains the mystery of the gospel: "God, who is rich in mercy, because of His great love that He had for us, made us alive with the Messiah even though we were dead in trespasses. You are saved by grace!" We may find the mystery of God to be confusing and frustrating when we encounter questions and circumstances that don't make sense. And yet our greatest blessing and the greatest story God has written is found in the mystery of the gospel.

REMEMBER THESE KEY THOUGHTS FROM THIS WEEK'S STUDY:

- The mystery of God is embedded in His creation and revealed in Christ.
- God's thoughts are higher than our thoughts and His ways are higher than our ways. That's what makes Him God.
- The mystery of God should lead us to worship.

God's mystery is closely tied to His holiness—the idea that God is not simply a bigger, better version of us. He is in a category entirely to Himself. Next week, we will explore God's holy, transcendent nature.

PURSUING GOD

NEPHILIM, MOSQUITOES, THE CROSS, AND OTHER UNSOLVED MYSTERIES

"My thoughts are nothing like your thoughts," says the LORD. "And my ways are far beyond anything you could imagine. For just as the heavens are higher than the earth, so my ways are higher than your ways and my thoughts higher than your thoughts." (Isaiah 55:8-9, NLT)

Personally, I've got tons of questions for God when I get to heaven. What the heck were the nephilim? Did You really create in just 6 days or did You do it over billions of years; and if so then how did all of the symbiotic relationships in nature develop? What happened to the 10 lost tribes of Israel? Why did You create mosquitoes and call them "good"?

What do you wish you understood better?

We might say, "God works in mysterious ways," but that is often just a polite way of asking, "Why does God do stuff that doesn't make sense?" There are so many things I would do differently. I would have never sent my son wrapped in the vulnerable skin of a baby and left him in the hands of a fallen people who had repeatedly proven their skillfulness at messing things up. And I sure wouldn't have left and entrusted the message of the kingdom to a bunch of people who denied it only 40 days earlier.

Let's think about the miracles for a moment. Imagine: Animals willingly and instinctually moved toward a big boat and climbed aboard. Huge walls crashed to the ground at the sound of a march, a shout, and a blast of the trumpet. A shepherd boy with no military training killed a giant. A virgin gave birth. And without question, the great mystery of our faith: Christ revealed in a human body and His death atonement for our sins. How does this happen?

.For centuries, theologians have offered up theories and metaphors to explain how it works. Scriptures have been exegeted and systematic theologies configured to explain it. But in the end, we are left with the unsettling realization that "systematic theology" doesn't cover everything. We can't quite grasp the shocking and unorthodox mystery of His ways. All we really know is that the blood of life pumped through Christ's beat-less heart.

How has Jesus' work on the cross changed your perception and understanding of God?

PURSUING GOD

"Once upon a time …" This phrase is the door into a land of mysteries. Throughout history we have embraced stories that teach us about a world beyond what we experience everyday and somehow usher us into that other world. In a sense, they tell us that other world is not too far off or too difficult to get to. The tales begin in an everyday way in an everyday place. Lonely Cinderella is doing her chores, Dorothy is still in Kansas, Lucy is playing an ordinary game of hide-and-seek on a boring summer afternoon. The fairy tale world invades the normal world as if to tell us to enter the extraordinary through the ordinary. The stories themselves don't feel the need to explain the transposing of places. The leap from one world to the next isn't seen as a leap at all but simply the next step on a casual afternoon walk.

The new world is unrecognizably strange. Is it safe? Is it dangerous? And almost as soon as the characters enter, they find a quest more important than anything they've ever known. They are uncomfortably ill-equipped; everything hinges on their ability to complete the impossible. Nothing is what it seems or appears to be. Trees come alive and witches look like the Fairy Godmother. Everything is in disguise, and somehow the hero of the story learns to distinguish truth from the tricks and tune into the small whisper that they've known all along. Like an artist, the story writer knows that the process is where the real adventure is found. The process is dangerous with near misses and close calls. It's costly, transformative, and necessary; and at the end, everything is revealed for what it really is.

Most of all, we love fairy tales because a great but seemingly insignificant good conquers the unconquerable evil. It is a world where terrible and wonderful and impossible things happen. The under-glorified part of the story is the cost at which victory is achieved. All great tales must have an element of the tragic. But before we can say "The End," the wicked get what they deserve, deception is brought into the light, the good rise to the occasion and pass the test into greatness. Everyone becomes known by their true name, even if that means they get a new name.

The Book of Ecclesiastes declares that God has planted eternity in our hearts. That's why we love these stories. The mystery of something wonderful we can't quite put our finger on is as near to us and as real as our heartbeat.

This is the mystery of the gospel: somehow, against all odds, there is victory. And in this life we find ourselves in the middle of a story that has not yet ended.

Reflect on a time when God invaded the reality of your life and completely turned your reality upside down. How did that experience change you?

PURSUING GOD

THE UPSIDE-DOWN KINGDOM

The upside-down kingdom is like a homeless man who leads a radical revolution in a powerful city where he overthrows the rich by creating a currency based on the everyday life of the poor.

The Beatitudes tell us that Christ's kingdom values are profoundly backwards, inside out, upside down. They are totally opposite to the values of the world. The world rewards power, comfort, recognition, success, and security.

Remember the handwriting on the wall? It is another kingdom mystery. Daniel tells us that the message written on the wall is "MENE, MENE, TEKEL, UPHARSIN." It meant the king had sought temporary satisfaction and his time was over. The writing on the wall is for the kingdom of the world: if you are living for yourself, then you are like King Belshazzar and your kingdom will dissolve. Invest in what is lasting.

When Christ comes on the scene, He preaches a radical kingdom that is fundamentally different from the world. The meek inherit the earth. The poor are actually the rich ones. To gain your life you must lose it. To be first you must become a slave. The kingdom of God must be entered as a child.

Jesus awakens our minds to the mystery of the kingdom of God. The climax of Christ's message leaves Him hanging on a cross, dying for a world that denied Him. In the life He lived, the Person He was, and what He accomplished, Christ is the revealer of mysteries and He is the mystery revealed.

The gospel is often called the "great reversal" because it is so mysterious and contradictory to our normal definition of good news. Part of the good news is that you must die to yourself, take up your cross, and follow. The Beatitudes give us the beautiful insight that earthly rewards can be replaced with heavenly ones. We all have the opportunity to make that exchange.

We must live our lives upside down, and there are far more mysteries in this kingdom yet to comprehend: How does the Trinity work? What is the mystery behind the Lord's Supper? C.S. Lewis said, "The command, after all, was 'Take and eat,' not, 'Take and understand.'" Some things will never be understood on this side of heaven.

There can be certainty in the mystery—it's called faith.

Read Matthew 5:1-11. Which of these statements is most challenging to you right now? Write out a prayer asking God to help you look more like Christ by living a life wrapped in the mystery of the upside-down kingdom.

HOLINESS

The attribute of God's holiness gets to the core of the question, *Who is God?* When God called Moses to liberate the Israelites from Pharaoh's oppression, Moses needed to explain to the Israelites what his mission was and Who sent him. He needed an explanation, some way to translate the voice and the authority behind the mysterious burning bush.

In Exodus 3:14, God introduced Himself to Moses as "I AM WHO I AM." He went on to say, "This is what you are to say to the Israelites: I AM has sent me to you." While that description lacked detail and didn't exactly solve Moses' dilemma to convince all of Israel with an impressive authority, "I AM" actually explained it all. "I AM" is the all-encompassing attribute that includes everything else about God. It's like God is saying, I AM the reason, I AM the author of this story and the main character. "I AM" packs in every other attribute we could possibly think to ascribe to God and thousands we cannot yet comprehend. "I AM," in all its mysteriousness and vagueness, tells us one thing—He is distinct from anything we know. He's wholly … other.

God is holy. There is a tendency to associate that word with goodness and perfection or righteousness. But what it means at its core is that God is set apart. He is utterly and wholly different from all His creation. There is none like Him. He is not simply a bigger, better version of us. He is in a category all to Himself.

We use a lot of words to describe God—just, merciful, gracious, omniscient, omnipotent, providential. But *holiness* is what we come to when we have used up all those words. Maybe that's why the soundtrack of heaven is a cosmic repeat of the refrain, "Holy, holy, holy is the Lord God Almighty." There is absolutely nothing more we can possibly say. But we dare not say less.

Use this time to talk with your group about how God has revealed Himself to you since last week's study.

From your devotional time last week, how did you answer the question: Reflect on a time when God invaded the reality of your life and completely turned your reality upside down. How did that experience change you?

Where has the mystery of God appeared in your life over the past week?

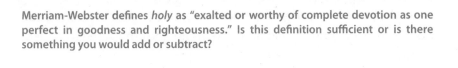
Merriam-Webster defines *holy* as "exalted or worthy of complete devotion as one perfect in goodness and righteousness." Is this definition sufficient or is there something you would add or subtract?

What people, places, or objects were designated as holy in Scripture?

Jesus says, "Be holy, because I am holy" (1 Peter 1:16). Do you think this command is possible or impossible? Why?

Fill in the blanks below on important points as you view the message from Mark. You'll unpack this information with the group after the video.

Your outlook on life is determined by your _____ _____

of who God is.

The word *holy* means absolutely _____.

The word *holy* means wholly _____.

A.W. Tozer said God's holiness is not simply the best we know infinitely bettered,

it is _____, _____, _____.[1]

Without the _____ of God, you cannot enter into

the _____ of God.

We underestimate the _____ of God because we underestimate

the _____ of God.

You won't see God seated on the throne if you're _____.

It's not until we completely submit our lives to the _____

of Jesus Christ that we have a revelation of His holiness.

1. *http://www.cmalliance.org/devotions/tozer?id=1422*

ISAIAH 6:1-3, ESV

In the year that King Uzziah died I saw the Lord sitting upon a throne, high and lifted up; and the train of his robe filled the temple. Above him stood the seraphim. Each had six wings: with two he covered his face, and with two he covered his feet, and with two he flew. And one called to another and said:

"Holy, holy, holy is the LORD of hosts;
the whole earth is full of his glory!"

ISAIAH 6:5

Then I said:

Woe is me for I am ruined

because I am a man of unclean lips

and live among a people of unclean lips,

and because my eyes have seen the King,

the LORD of Hosts.

JOSHUA 24:19

He is a holy God.

- The image that comes to mind most often when we think about God should be one of Him seated on the throne because that's where He is.
- The character of God is interrelated. If you don't have a full comprehension of the holiness of God, you are not going to understand the love of God or the mercy of God.
- Until we understand the depravity of the sin in our hearts, we can't possibly appreciate the amazing grace and mercy that God is showing.
- The word *hallow* literally means to keep a thing holy in your heart.

Mark mentions that we can't have the mercy of God without the holiness of God and the way to recapture holiness is to keep God holy in our hearts. What are some actions and attitudes we can practice to keep God holy in our hearts?

SMALL-GROUP DIALOGUE—

What comes to mind when you think about God? What framed pictures are hanging on the walls of your mind? You need to intentionally frame pictures of God in your mind. There are two dominant images of God framed in my mind. One is a picture of Jesus standing at the door knocking, a visual image of Revelation 3:20 where He says: "Listen! I stand at the door and knock." The other picture is an image of Jesus with a lamb draped around His neck. Those images are dominant for me because those two pictures hung in my grandparents' home. As a little kid, those images were engraved on my mind.

What picture of Jesus is dominant in your mind?

The Bible is replete with images of God, and Isaiah 6 gives us a snapshot that is very different from the polite Jesus at the door and the tranquil Shepherd in the field.

ISAIAH 6:1-4

In the year that King Uzziah died, I saw the Lord seated on a high and lofty throne, and His robe filled the temple. Seraphim were standing above Him; each one had six wings: with two he covered his face, with two he covered his feet, and with two he flew. And one called to another:

> *Holy, holy, holy is the Lord of Hosts;*
>
> *His glory fills the whole earth.*

The foundations of the doorways shook at the sound of their voices, and the temple was filled with smoke.

As you read this description of God's throne, how does it compare with the mental image you have of heaven?

This passage is strikingly similar to John's vision of God's throne as recorded in Revelation 4:6-8, where we read that the worship of God is never-ending. Revelation tells us that the choirs of heaven sing praises, "Holy, holy, holy, Lord God, the Almighty, who was, who is, and who is coming." And then they repeat that. And repeat it again. And again. For all eternity. Sometimes I wonder what could possibly be pleasing to God about listening to a broken record. Or how long that can really be meaningful. Evidently there is something about the holiness of God that inspires and requires unbounded and unlimited worship.

What do these passages teach you about worship?

How might we engage in continual worship through the way we live our lives?

Let's go back to the story of Isaiah.

ISAIAH 6:5-7

Then I said:

> *Woe is me for I am ruined*
>
> *because I am a man of unclean lips*
>
> *and live among a people of unclean lips,*
>
> *and because my eyes have seen the King,*
>
> *the Lord of Hosts.*

Then one of the seraphim flew to me, and in his hand was a glowing coal that he had taken from the altar with tongs. He touched my mouth with it and said:

> *Now that this has touched your lips,*
>
> *your wickedness is removed*
>
> *and your sin is atoned for.*

Read about Isaiah's encounter in Isaiah 6:5-7. How do you think we can put ourselves in a position to have an encounter like this? Or is this out of our control?

What happens when humanity encounters the holiness of God?

Like Isaiah, we need a revelation of the holiness of God. I'm not entirely sure how we do that, but I do know we won't see God seated on His throne as long as we are trying to stand on the throne of our own lives. We cannot get a revelation of God unless we are on our knees or flat on our faces. The only way we see God high and exalted is if we go low and humble. The more time we spend on our knees with our eyes closed, the clearer picture we will have of God seated on His throne.

We need a posture of humility and submission in order to see the holiness of God, and once we see His holiness, it will cause us to humble ourselves and submit even further. Maybe that's why the heavenly creatures never stop declaring His holiness; with every bow to the throne, they see a new dimension of His holiness that causes them to bow down once again.

How would you define the words *humility* and *submission*?

List two or three practical actions you can take this week to put you in a position to see the holiness of God.

What are some ways in which you have made God into your own image?

What were the consequences?

ISAIAH 6:8

Then I heard the voice of the Lord saying:

> *Who should I send?*

> *Who will go for Us?*

I said:

> *Here I am. Send me.*

When the Great I Am speaks, I think the only appropriate response is "Here I am. Send me."

There seems to be a connection between confession and calling in this passage. As Isaiah postures himself in humility, God positions Isaiah for his calling. How do you ensure that you posture yourself before God instead of positioning yourself before men?

Later in the Book of Isaiah, God declares, "As heaven is higher than earth, so My ways are higher than your ways, and My thoughts than your thoughts" (55:9). One of our greatest dangers is to make God in our own image and then get confused about why we don't understand His ways.

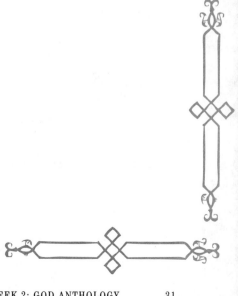

WRAP ———————————

When we comprehend God's holiness, we learn that He is wholly other. He is wholly good, wholly worthy of praise, and wholly different from us.

REMEMBER THESE KEY THOUGHTS FROM THIS WEEK'S STUDY:

- God is not simply a bigger, better version of us. He is set apart and wholly other.
- When we encounter God's holiness, it will lead to worship.
- To get a revelation of God's holiness, we must take on a posture of humility and submission.
- We must focus more on posturing ourselves before God than positioning ourselves before men.

The Lord's Prayer (Matthew 6:9-13) begins with an acknowledgment of God's holiness. As you close your group study this week, pray this prayer together, making this a time of reflection.

Our Father in heaven,

Your name be honored as holy.

Your kingdom come.

Your will be done

on earth as it is in heaven.

Give us today our daily bread.

And forgive us our debts,

as we also have forgiven our debtors.

And do not bring us into temptation,

but deliver us from the evil one.

For Yours is the kingdom and the power

and the glory forever. Amen.

PURSUING GOD

What we think about God is the most important thing about us. What we embrace as truth and believe in faith will affect the way we live. That is why the Bible tells us to renew our minds and put on the helmet of truth. We must think about God rightly or we will worship a god of our own creation and be conformed to the likeness of an idol.

A low view of God reflects a cynical, embittered, frightened, jealous, and self-centered heart and forces us to try to fill God's shoes, rendering us our own lower-case "g" gods. On the other hand, a high view of God will result in a deeper relationship with Him, greater faith, faithful stewardship, deeper trust, awe in His character, and eyes to see His beauty. A high view of God puts God in His rightful place in our lives and ensures that we posture ourselves in the right place before Him.

To have a high view of God, we turn to the dimensions of His character as revealed in Scripture. There are more than 400 names for God in Scripture, and each reveals a different dimension of who He is. Throughout the rest of eternity, we will never cease to discover all He is or come to the end of His worthiness.

Read Psalm 18. Make a list of all the attributes and names of God that you find in that passage.

Identify the two that mean the most to you right now in your life. Why are they so special to you?

PURSUING GOD

Throughout the Bible, the "law" is consistently referenced. In Psalm 119, David declares, "I delight in your law." The prophets of the Old Testament urged people to come back to the Lawgiver and follow His laws. In the New Testament, the Pharisees and Sadducees were experts in the law. The instructions in Leviticus comprise a significant part of this oft-mentioned law, including specifics of what constitutes sin, how to offer acceptable sacrifices, and how to conduct religious ceremonies. These instructions for right living are unbelievably complex by any standard, and yet Leviticus 20:26 hints at why all this is here. It states, "You are to be holy to Me because I, Yahweh, am holy."

All the crazy rules are actually telling us something about who God is. They are telling us about the purity of holiness, and they say that God intends to make us like Him.

This process, becoming like God (specifically the Person of Christ), is called sanctification. His holiness expresses itself in shaping us from hesitant followers into full-fledged kingdom builders with all the descriptors of Himself: patient, brave, loving, humble yet confident, foolishly unselfish and generous, hospitable, and remarkably honest and authentic. Essentially, we come by none of these characteristics naturally. That is why the most powerful testimonies have not so much to do with what people were saved from, but what they were saved to. The most powerful stories point to what becomes of our lives after conversion.

When we share our testimony, the story of what God has done in our lives, we often focus on the sordid details of what God has saved us *from*. But that is only half of the story. What has God saved you *to*?

The obvious hang-up is that we often look and feel anything but holy. Leviticus doesn't give us an impossible command to accomplish; rather, it shows us how the impossible is accomplished. It teaches us the crazy and mysterious notion that something perfect can transform the imperfect. The unclean can become clean. The unholy can become holy, as He is holy.

PURSUING GOD

We insist on creating a god in our image. Logic alone tells us our mortal, finite, limited abilities would produce a tiny, small, finite god. We make God out to be nothing more than superhuman—a bigger, better version of us. Something remarkable happened to Moses when he encountered the voice behind the burning bush. He had an experience with "I AM."

Consider the people who encountered God and His holiness: Moses' face radiated; Isaiah saw the Lord on His throne; Abraham left his community to follow an unknown God to an unknown place; Daniel openly and boldly followed God in a harsh culture; Stephen was stoned as he gazed into heaven.

It seems that the men and women who experienced the divine learned one very crucial lesson: they learned to pray and act according to who God is and not according to their potential. It was their humanity that left them tongue-tied, far from home, facing accusations, and in a lion's den.

What is a situation you are currently facing in which you need to start praying and acting according to who God is and not according to your potential? Write out a simple prayer here:

Christ embodies holiness. He is the One who Colossians 1 says "is the image of the invisible God. … For God was pleased to have all His fullness dwell in Him" (vv. 15,19). When people experience Christ on earth, it becomes earth as it is in heaven: He heals, feeds, forgives, casts away demons, teaches, befriends, transforms.

As Christians, we are told to let our minds be transformed. To think on what is pure, good, and lovely. In a nutshell, we are told to set our minds on what is holy. We are to experience Christ. We are called to divine thoughts and to live according to Him.

SESSION THREE

INCOMPARABILITY

More than a century ago, Albert Einstein published what may be the most recognizable equation in the realm of science: $e = mc^2$. Energy equals mass multiplied by the speed of light squared. Now, the speed of light squared is a very large number. Let me translate it simply: there is an awful lot of energy in a very small amount of matter. In fact, the amount of potential energy in every invisible atom is almost inconceivable.

If the amount of energy in every subatomic particle is virtually inconceivable, then how can we even begin to comprehend the potential energy of an omnipotent Creator who created all matter? We can't.

In the beginning, God created us in His image, but we've been creating God in our image ever since. We cannot conceive of anything beyond our four dimensions of space time, so we project our four dimensions of spacetime limitations on God and conjure up a god who is a little bigger, a little better, a little stronger, and a little wiser than we are. We tend to think that God's power is slightly more powerful than the most powerful thing we can imagine. We tend to think of God's grace as slightly more gracious than the most gracious thing we can imagine. We tend to think of God's wisdom as slightly wiser than the wisest person we've ever known.

When we turn to the Scriptures, however, we find that God is incomparably wise, gracious, loving, and powerful. There is absolutely no comparison between God and us. He is not a little bit bigger, a little bit better, a little bit stronger, a little bit wiser; He is so much more than that.

Use this time to talk with your group about how God has revealed Himself to you since last week's study.

In what ways have you engaged worship differently since our discussion on holiness last week?

How can our view of God's holiness practically impact our lives on a daily basis?

What are some ways you have made God in your own image?

What is the biggest way God has revealed Himself in your life or in the life of someone close to you?

Fill in the blanks below on important points as you view the message from Mark. You'll unpack this information with the group after the video.

God's power is not just incomparable. His power isn't just great. His power is

_____ _____.

In order to comprehend God's incomparable love, grace, and power,

we need _____. We need to get into His _____

and into His _____ and ask Him to reveal it to us.

While God's power is measureless, the prophet Isaiah gives us a glimpse of His

omnipotence by comparing it to the size of the _____.

Even the most brilliant among us underestimate God by _____.

EPHESIANS 1:17-19, NIV

I keep asking that the God of our Lord Jesus Christ, the glorious Father, may give you the Spirit of wisdom and revelation, so that you may know him better. I pray also that the eyes of your heart may be enlightened in order that you may know the hope to which he has called you, the riches of his glorious inheritance in the saints, and his incomparably great power for us who believe. That power is like the working of his mighty strength.

ISAIAH 55:9, NIV

As the heavens are higher than the earth,

so are my ways higher than your ways

and my thoughts than your thoughts.

- If the amount of energy in every subatomic particle is virtually inconceivable, then how can we even begin to comprehend the potential energy of the omnipotent Creator who created all matter?
- God cannot be compared to anything.
- Your best thought on your best day falls 15.5 billion light-years short of how great and how good God really is.

Take a moment to pray together the prayer of Paul in Ephesians 1:17-19.

SMALL-GROUP DIALOGUE—

One of our biggest problems is a small view of God. Every other problem is a by-product of bringing God down to our level. Ultimately, our perspective is off if our problems seem bigger than God.

When Paul wrote to the church at Ephesus, he prayed a prayer that included some theological perspective for them to cling to.

EPHESIANS 1:16-19

I never stop giving thanks for you as I remember you in my prayers. I pray that the God of our Lord Jesus Christ, the glorious Father, would give you a spirit of wisdom and revelation in the knowledge of Him. I pray that the perception of your mind may be enlightened so you may know what is the hope of His calling, what are the glorious riches of His inheritance among the saints, and what is the immeasurable greatness of His power to us who believe, according to the working of His vast strength.

The NIV translates "immeasurable" as "incomparable." Paul says God's power is not just great, God's power is not just incomparable, he says God's power is incomparably great. In other words, there is no point of comparison.

What does Paul pray for the members of the church in Ephesus and what does this possibly reveal about his presupposition of these members?

During what circumstances or seasons of life have you sensed God changing your perception of His character and capabilities?

Consider the problems in your life right now that seem bigger than God. How can you change that perception?

Last week I mentioned that what comes to mind when we think about God is the most important thing about us. I talked about a couple of images that come to my mind when I think about Jesus. Sometimes I imagine Him standing at a door knocking. It's a depiction of Revelation 3:20. Other times I picture Him in a serene pastoral landscape with a sheep around His shoulders—a depiction of Jesus as the Good Shepherd.

Considering last week's discussion on holiness, what is now the dominant image that comes to your mind when you think about Jesus?

For many of us, the dominant mental image of Jesus is Him hanging on the cross. That is the crux of our faith; that is where the love of God is painted blood red; and it's a sacred picture. I'm so thankful for that picture. For what had to be the longest day of His life, He suffered, He sacrificed, and He gave us a picture of what love is.

As important as those images are, Paul gives a different image:

EPHESIANS 1:20-23

He demonstrated this power in the Messiah by raising Him from the dead and seating Him at His right hand in the heavens—far above every ruler and authority, power and dominion, and every title given, not only in this age but also in the one to come. And He put everything under His feet and appointed Him as head over everything for the church, which is His body, the fullness of the One who fills all things in every way.

Right now Jesus is not hanging on a cross. He is seated on a throne. That's not an image we see depicted very often, and because we don't have the mental image of Jesus sitting in power and authority, it robs the victory from us before we even pray. I wonder if our greatest shortcoming is how much we underestimate the authority of Christ and the authority we have because we are in Christ.

Paul mentions the authority we have because we are in Christ. Scripture is ripe with promises of this authority and pictures of faithful people operating in that authority. What instances can you recall from Scripture that remind you of the victory we have in Christ?

How might the awareness of this authority affect the way you live?

How big is your God? Is He bigger than your sin? "Where sin multiplied, grace multiplied even more" (Romans 5:20). Is He bigger than your addiction? Jesus said, "He has sent Me to proclaim freedom to the captives" (Luke 4:18). Is He bigger than whatever kind of physical problem you have? "We are healed by His wounds" (Isaiah 53:5). Is God bigger than the trials and hardships we face? Yes! Most of us would give mental assent to the beliefs that God is Savior, Deliverer, and Healer, but it's just so much easier to believe God for the impersonal big stuff like keeping the planets in orbit than the little personal stuff like our problems. Paul referenced the life-giving and resurrection power of the Spirit in his letter to the Romans, as well.

ROMANS 8:11

If the Spirit of Him who raised Jesus from the dead lives in you, then He who raised Christ from the dead will also bring your mortal bodies to life through His Spirit who lives in you.

We've got to add God into the equation of our lives. God is seated far above every power, rule, and authority, but how do we appropriate that to our lives? What difference does that make to us? In Ephesians 1:1-19, Paul prays for a spirit of wisdom and revelation. He says, "I pray that the perception of your mind may be enlightened so you may know what is the hope of His calling, what are the glorious riches of His inheritance among the saints, and what is the immeasurable greatness of His power to us who believe, according to the working of His vast strength" (vv. 18-19). You can't reason your way to God. It will not get you there. Reason is a wonderful thing, but it will only take you as far as the hundred billion synapses that you have.

At some point, reasonableness isn't enough. We need revelation. It's revelation, not reason, that will help us come to terms with the incomparable God. Revelation goes beyond logic. It's not illogical as some suggest. It's simply theological. It adds God into the equation. When we filter God's capabilities through our logic, we lose sight of His purpose. But when we add God and His inconceivable greatness into the equation, all bets are off.

Do you tend to reason your way to revelation or allow revelation to shape your reasoning? Discuss the difference.

Describe a moment where God worked in a way that defied your logic.

WRAP ————

We have a tendency to confine God to the dimensions of the world we live in. But God is not the product of creation; He is the Creator. His greatness cannot be calculated by our standards and cannot be measured by our means. He is the incomparable God.

REMEMBER THESE KEY THOUGHTS FROM THIS WEEK'S STUDY:

- God's power is incomparably great.
- One of our biggest problems is our small view of God.
- Jesus is not hanging on the cross; He is seated at the right hand of the Father.
- When you add God to the equation of your life, all bets are off.

As you close out your group gathering this week, agree with this prayer of A.W. Tozer from his book *Knowledge of the Holy*:

Lord, how great is our dilemma! In Thy Presence silence best becomes us, but love inflames our hearts and constrains us to speak. Were we to hold our peace the stones would cry out; yet if we speak, what shall we say? Teach us to know that we cannot know, for the things of God knoweth no man, but the Spirit of God. Let faith support us where reason fails, and we shall think because we believe, not in order that we may believe. In Jesus' name. Amen.[1]

Next week we will explore the mercy of God. It's one of His attributes that we are least likely to question yet proves to be difficult to fully comprehend.

1. A.W. Tozer, *Knowledge of the Holy* (New York: HarperCollins Publishers, 1961), 6.

PURSUING GOD

I will praise You because I have been remarkably and wonderfully made. Your works are wonderful, and I know this very well. (Psalm 139:14)

There never has been and never will be anyone like you. But that isn't a testament to you. It's a testament to the God who created you absolutely unique. If God's power, presence, and wisdom are incomparable, it means His creation can be incomparably diverse.

Jesus said that if we remain silent the stones will cry out (see Luke 19:40). All of creation is singing a worship chorus to God. The meadowlark sings with a range of 300 notes. The nightingale finch has a repertoire of 24 songs. According to the German physicist and pianist Arnold Summerfield, a hydrogen atom emits 100 frequencies, making it more complex musically than a grand piano, which emits 88 frequencies.

Because no one else was created just like you, no one else can worship just like you. Think about this: what might be one specific way that you are designed to worship God like no one else?

All of creation is singing a unique song to the Creator, and you are part of that universal chorus. No one can worship God for you or like you because God has given you a unique voiceprint. There are millions of people praying and worshiping God in every language all the time, but your voiceprint is unique. Like a parent who knows his child's unique cry or scream or laugh, God knows your voice, hears your voice, and loves your voice. You are uniquely wired to worship God like nothing else in all creation can. That alone is enough to keep us praising His immeasurable greatness throughout eternity.

PURSUING GOD

BIG VIEW OF A BIG GOD

"My thoughts are not your thoughts, and your ways are not My ways." This is the LORD's declaration. *"For as heaven is higher than earth, so My ways are higher than your ways, and My thoughts than your thoughts."* (Isaiah 55:8-9)

On a bad day, we tend to reduce God to the size of our greatest failure, problem, or fear. On a good day, we reduce God to the size of our greatest gift, highest hope, or best attribute. However, Scripture reveals that God is infinitely better than your best thought on your best day.

When God enters the equation, anything is possible. It's not about what you can do for God but about what the incomparable God can do in you and through you. With God, anything is possible. A couple of fish and a handful of bread become a miraculous feast for five thousand. A slingshot and a stone become the weapons that save a nation.

Few moments are more thrilling than doing what you didn't think could be done. And it's not just thrilling for you. It's thrilling for God. Like a proud parent, our heavenly Father loves it when we do the impossible by His power and for His glory. When you live in raw dependence upon His immeasurable greatness and His incomparable power, you will see God do the impossible.

Think about a seemingly insurmountable challenge in your life right now. Write out a prayer that reflects a faith rooted in God's immeasurable greatness. Then write one action step you can take this week to engage that challenge.

PURSUING GOD

"Who will you compare Me to, or who is My equal?" asks the Holy One. (Isaiah 40:25)

Several years ago I was in Southern California with my two brothers-in-law, Joel and Rob. Joel is about my size. Rob is a little bigger. Actually, he is a lot bigger. The three of us wanted to go boogie boarding, but the water was really cold. A friend of ours found some wetsuits for us to borrow. One minor detail presented a potential problem: our friend borrowed the wet suits from three junior high kids. I am not exaggerating when I tell you it took me 10 minutes to pull that wetsuit on. (Granted, I wasted a lot of that time by initially putting the wet suit on backwards.) Finally, Joel and I managed to squeeze ourselves into our suits.

We turned around to find that Rob hadn't even pushed his arms through the armholes yet. His hands wouldn't even fit. This is embarrassing, and I probably shouldn't admit it, but this was the first (and hopefully last) time Joel and I have ever dressed Rob. We finally got the suit on him, but there was no way we could zip up the back. And so Rob marched toward the waves with a V-backed wet suit.

As we rode the first wave, the inevitable happened. Rob's suit filled with water, and he sank like an anchor. I have rarely laughed that hard in my life. There *is* a spiritual point to this story.

How many times have we tried to stuff God into the spiritual equivalent of a junior high wet suit? We try to bring God down to our level, as if God can fit within the constraints of our left brain or the confines of our imagination. It's ridiculous. If it wasn't so sad and detrimental to our spiritual health, it might be funny. Instead, it kills our faith, our hope, and our joy.

Take a moment to review the Scripture passages from this week's study on the massiveness of God. Choose one to commit to memory and write it here:

SESSION FOUR

MERCY

Soon after God created humankind, we disobeyed His commands and separated ourselves from Him, incurring a debt we could not repay and earning for ourselves a most grievous punishment.

But God didn't demand that we repay the debt. He satisfied it Himself. When Jesus, the Messiah, the Son of God, hung on a Roman cross, He bore the judgment that was due to the world. The power of the cross and its demonstration of mercy lie not in ridding God of His justice or wrath. Those are very much alive and well. Rather, Jesus took upon Himself our punishment and pain in the greatest act of love and mercy the world would ever know.

My wife, Lora, bought me a hammock for Father's Day one year. I have to admit that I experienced a little trouble getting positioned in it the first time. I put one leg in and before I knew what happened, my back smacked the ground hard. But once I positioned myself correctly, I was able to rest peacefully.

The mercy of God is like a hammock. A hammock where you rest all of your body weight in the wonderful grace of God. The problem is that we often lean only partially into it and flip ourselves out. But when we get into that hammock and rest in the mercy of God, there is nothing like it.

God wants to show us His mercy. What we have to do is learn to rest in it, not by human striving or even by our good works; it is simply by the grace of God that we are saved, and in that we can find a spiritual rest unlike any other rest we can experience.

Lamentations 3:22-23 promises that "His mercies never end. They are new every morning." One of the greatest, most generous promises in all of Scripture.

Use this time to talk with your group about how God has revealed Himself to you since last week's study.

How is your image of God developing over the course of this study?

What are some big, impossible prayers you are praying that you could share with the group?

Describe a time when someone showed mercy to you or you showed mercy to someone else.

When you see a picture of the cross, do you associate Jesus' sacrifice with wrath or mercy? Explain.

Fill in the blanks below on important points as you view the message from Mark. You'll unpack this information with the group after the video.

Mercy is like a _____, where you rest all of your body weight in the wonderful _____ of God.

The word *Lord* translated in the Old Testament is the name "Elohim" and it denotes the _____ of God. The word *God* is the Hebrew word "Jehovah" which denotes His _____.

_____ activates the mercy of God.

Mercy is God _____ _____ what we deserve and *grace* is God _____ us what we don't deserve.

We can approach the throne of grace with _____.

MICAH 6:6,8, NIV

With what shall I come before the LORD

and bow down before the exalted God? …

He has showed you, O man, what is good.

And what does the LORD require of you?

To act justly and to love mercy

and to walk humbly with your God.

HEBREWS 4:16, NIV

Let us then approach the throne of grace with confidence, so that we may receive mercy and find grace to help us in our time of need.

EXODUS 20:5-6

I, the LORD your God, am a jealous God, punishing the children for the fathers' sin, to the third and fourth generations of those who hate Me, but showing faithful love to a thousand generations of those who love Me and keep My commands.

- God always wants to show mercy.
- If you don't go to the throne of grace you'll end up at the judgment throne. But God invites us to approach the throne of grace so that we might obtain mercy and receive grace.
- God's attribute of mercy exceeds His attribute of justice by 500 fold.
- There is no end to His mercy. He never runs out of mercy. His mercies are new every morning.

Mark defined *mercy* as God withholding from us what we deserve and *grace* as God giving us what we don't deserve. What are some practical examples of God's mercy and grace in your life?

SMALL-GROUP DIALOGUE—

There are over 400 names for God referenced in Scripture and each one reveals a different part of His personality. The word *Lord* translated in the Old Testament is the name "Elohim" and it denotes the mercy of God. The name *God* is the Hebrew word "Jehovah," which denotes His justice. Many times, the two words are used together: "Lord God."

Sometimes truth is found in the tension of opposites. How do you think God's mercy and judgment work together?

As we turn to the New Testament, we find that Jesus gives us a tangible picture of the mercy of the Father. In John's Gospel, Jesus never utters the word *mercy*, but He gives us one of the most poignant and potent pictures of mercy. One of my core values is to love people when they least expect it and least deserve it. This story is a powerful example of that value expressed through Jesus.

JOHN 8:3-11

Then the scribes and the Pharisees brought a woman caught in adultery, making her stand in the center. "Teacher," they said to Him, "this woman was caught in the act of committing adultery. In the law Moses commanded us to stone such women. So what do You say?" They asked this to trap Him, in order that they might have evidence to accuse Him.

Jesus stooped down and started writing on the ground with His finger. When they persisted in questioning Him, He stood up and said to them, "The one without sin among you should be the first to throw a stone at her."

Then He stooped down again and continued writing on the ground. When they heard this, they left one by one, starting with the older men. Only He was left, with the woman in the center. When Jesus stood up, He said to her, "Woman, where are they? Has no one condemned you?"

"No one, Lord," she answered.

"Neither do I condemn you," said Jesus. "Go, and from now on do not sin anymore."

Which character do you identify with most in this story: the woman or the Pharisees? Why?

Consider what you know about Jesus. What do you think He was scribbling in the sand?

Death was the rightful punishment for adultery according to Old Testament law. Furthermore, God hates adultery because it tears relationships apart and rips the fabric of God's image as displayed through the marriage relationship. Yet Jesus shows mercy. What limits the extent of God's mercy?

The Pharisees responded to Jesus by dropping their rocks and walking away. Jesus responded to the woman that she was not condemned so she should go and not sin. The mercy of God demands a response from us. We can either walk away in dejected bitterness or we can strive to look more like Christ. The Old Testament prophet Micah gives us some insight into God's heart and expectations.

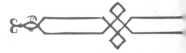

MICAH 6:6-8

With what shall I come before the Lord

  and bow down before the exalted God?

Shall I come before him with burnt offerings,

  with calves a year old?

Will the Lord be pleased with thousands of rams,

  with ten thousand rivers of olive oil?

Shall I offer my firstborn for my transgression,

  the fruit of my body for the sin of my soul?

He has shown you, O mortal, what is good.

  And what does the Lord require of you?

To act justly and to love mercy

  and to walk humbly with your God. (NIV)

What three responses does the Lord require of us? What do you think makes such a simple command so difficult?

What do the traits of justice, mercy, and humility have in common?

Describe a situation you are currently facing in which you could demonstrate mercy in a very tangible way. Don't hold back; show someone mercy like it has been shown to you.

Mercy is not just a blessing God bestows on others or a characteristic He requires of us. As we have already read, His mercies are new every morning. Jesus invites us to come into His presence. As the perfect high priest, He is in the unique position of understanding us and granting us forgiveness.

HEBREWS 4:14-16

Since we have a great high priest who has passed through the heavens—Jesus the Son of God—let us hold fast to the confession. For we do not have a high priest who is unable to sympathize with our weaknesses, but One who has been tested in every way as we are, yet without sin. Therefore let us approach the throne of grace with boldness, so that we may receive mercy and find grace to help us at the proper time.

We often think of mercy and grace as synonyms, but there is actually a wonderful distinction between the two. Mercy is God holding back what we deserve, while grace is God giving us what we don't deserve. We receive God's mercy when He protects us from death and hell through the cross. God's grace extends to us when He adopts us as sons and daughters into His family. When God shows mercy to us, the right response is to show mercy to others.

Identify moments of mercy and grace from the Scriptures and from your own life.

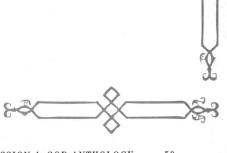

Mercy comes after confession. Why do you think God requires confession in order for us to receive mercy?

WRAP ———

God's mercy is a rescue from a just and deserved outcome. Throughout the Old and New Testaments, we see God displaying His mercy to His people in shocking and perplexing ways. Our response is to show mercy to other people.

REMEMBER THESE KEY THOUGHTS FROM THIS WEEK'S STUDY:

- Jesus took our punishment and our pain in the greatest act of love and mercy the world would ever know.
- God's love is like a hammock. We can rest all of the weight of our sin in it.
- God's mercies are new every morning.
- God desires that we love mercy more than we make sacrifice.
- Mercy is God holding back what we deserve. Grace is God giving us a blessing that we don't deserve.

Next week we will explore the jealousy of God. While we often think of jealousy as a negative character trait, God's jealousy is rooted in goodness and works for our good.

PURSUING GOD

God is merciful and just.

The tension between God's mercy and God's justice is one spot where the gospel gets confusing and sometimes even frustrating. We want to believe in a merciful God. Not a judging God. Not a God who would bring punishment or wrath or require sacrifices. What we are really describing is a passive god.

God forgives, He doesn't excuse. Sin does not become less costly or less hurtful because of mercy; through mercy it is God who assumes the expense. That is the crucial difference. A god who never judges is not in the position to grant mercy.

The definition of *sin* is "missing the mark." We will never see the wonders of mercy nor the depravity of sin until we see them both against the Person of God. Only a judge—someone in the rightful and legal position with authority, responsibility, and liability to bring punishment—is in the true and appropriate place to grant mercy.

We must see mercy as what it is: a rescue from a just and deserved outcome. The mercy of the cross is not that God's wrath on our sin is abolished, but that His wrath is satisfied by Someone other than the guilty party. Christ instead of us. That is the shocking mercy of the gospel. We begin to find that God's wrath is not too cruel, but that He is unimaginably good. Mercy is the insane notion that a substitute can and has been sacrificed in our place.

Think of a few places where you have missed the mark of God's perfection recently. Write a prayer asking for God's grace and mercy in those actions.

God is just. There are consequences to sin, but the guilty don't have to take it— He chooses to.

When Jesus of Nazareth came on the scene, John the Baptist recognized Him and proclaimed: "Here is the Lamb of God, who takes away the sin of the world!" (John 1:29).

God is not cruel in His justice. He is overwhelmingly merciful.

PURSUING GOD

Do not remember the sins of my youth or my acts of rebellion; in keeping with Your faithful love, remember me because of Your goodness, LORD. (Psalm 25:7)

Running from the authorities, Jean Valjean sought refuge in the home of the Bishop of Digne. The humble clergyman fed the escaped convict and gave him a place to stay. In the middle of the night, Valjean repaid the man's kindness by stealing his silver and running. When the police caught him and dragged him back before the priest, Valjean maintained that the silver had been a gift. The bishop confirmed the story and chastised Valjean for leaving behind the most precious pieces—two silver candlesticks. The bishop encouraged Valjean to make a new life for himself. Victor Hugo's classic *Les Misérables* is a story of both mercy (withholding judgment from one who deserves it) and grace (giving a blessing to one who doesn't deserve it).

While Valjean ran from judgment, mercy ran toward him. It reminds me of a similar story that Jesus told His disciples to help them understand the heart of the Father. In the Book of Matthew, Jesus spins a masterpiece of a story about a young man who demanded his inheritance and ran away to live a life of freedom and fun. Only the freedom and fun he hoped for never materialized and he found himself eating the same slop he was feeding the pigs he cared for.

We often find ourselves in the same shoes as the prodigal son referenced above. We pursue a promise of freedom only to find ourselves enslaved. Write about one of your prodigal son moments.

When the prodigal son finally came to his senses, he set out for home and rehearsed how he would beg for mercy from his father. But mercy always has a way of shocking us. He didn't have to beg for mercy—mercy came running as his father met him on the road and wrapped his son up in his arms. Mercy runs. That's how much God loves us.

PURSUING GOD

The Bible does not avoid the flaws in its characters. It even goes so far as to call these characters —with their nakedness and lying and adultery—heroes. Let's scroll through the heroes of the faith in Hebrews 11.

Abraham told Pharaoh his wife was his sister. Gideon and Noah had a bad ending. Rahab was a prostitute. Jacob was a deceiver. Samson fell into sexual sin. Sarah didn't believe God. Joseph was the bragging little brother. David slept with a married woman and killer her husband. The Israelites are likened to idolaters and adulterers. Jonah was put in a grand "time out." The list could continue throughout the entire Bible. Saul killed Christians. Peter was disloyal. Judas betrayed Jesus. The disciples weren't exactly contributing members of Jesus' team. In His greatest moment of need, they fell asleep!

As it turns out, the people in the Bible are just people like us with bruises and scars, who made bad choices (and some good ones), felt rejected, were afraid, unqualified, a little thickheaded, and a little prideful.

But these stories are not about the characters. They are testimony to who God is—a God of mercy. He did not come to save those who pretend to have it all together. He did not come for people who think they can save themselves. He came for people who know their need for Him. That might be the type of person He is most drawn to—those who know they desperately and urgently require His mercy. He came for the sole and single purpose of being mercy to a world of desperate, imperfect people.

If we want an example of mercy, we can look at Christ. The mercy of God and the miracle of Christ is that He "put on" our mess, so to speak. He related to it. He is the great prodigal father who picks up His cloak and runs—against all expectations and in spite of the distance—to His sons. And He throws them a party.

It might be in the party where we see the mercy of God most clearly. The party is when He gives us something to contribute. When we come to Him expecting to be slaves, He makes us sons. He brings us into His redemptive plan where reconciliation is just the beginning of the story.

Imagine that you headed into a situation in which you expect to be a slave only to learn that you are being adopted. Use the space below to describe your reaction.

SESSION FIVE

JEALOUSY

On Mount Sinai, God clearly and concisely revealed a shocking and seemingly base dimension of His character: "I, the LORD your God, am a jealous God" (Exodus 20:5). He repeated it for good measure 14 chapters later: "For the LORD, whose name is Jealous, is a jealous God" (34:14, NIV).

Jealousy typically has a negative connotation, so let me make a distinction. God is certainly not jealous of anything. He can't be; He is God. But God is jealous for something, and there is a difference between jealous of and jealous for. God is jealous for everything He created because it rightfully belongs to Him. Specifically, God is jealous for us. He is jealous for our love, our time, our devotion, and ultimately, our hearts. Why is God jealous for us? Because He infinitely loves us. His jealousy is an expression of His love.

When we begin to understand who God is—how long and high and wide and deep and good and majestic He is—we realize that God is worthy of all honor and all glory and all praise. We begin to recognize His incomparability, and we see that when Scripture teaches us that God is jealous, it's not unjust as ours so often is. He desires complete devotion and total dedication because He is worthy, because He is the reason we exist. And so, all we are and all we have we owe to Him.

God desires our recognition for His holiness, requiring of us our first and full affection. God's jealousy demands our faithfulness.

Our God is jealous for us.

Use this time to talk with your group about how God has revealed Himself to you since last week's study.

One outcome of studying the character of God should be that we begin to look more like Him. How did last week's study on mercy affect the way you look at and relate to other people—especially those who least deserve and expect love?

Share your response to the devotional activity: Imagine that you headed into a situation in which you expect to be a slave only to learn that you are being adopted. Describe your reaction.

Consider the statement, God is jealous. What kind of emotions or reactions do you have to that idea?

Is there such a thing as unselfish and pure jealousy? If so, how is that different from jealousy as we typically understand it?

Fill in the blanks below on important points as you view the message from Mark. You'll unpack this information with the group after the video.

We don't appreciate the _____ of God because we don't understand

the _____ of God.

God is not jealous _____ anything. But He is jealous _____ you.

What provokes God's jealousy? Anything that diverts our _____

or our _____ to someone or something else.

If you want to know if something is an idol, gauge your _____.

If Jesus is not Lord _____ all, He is not Lord _____ all.

EZEKIEL 8:3,5,7,10,12,14, NIV

The Spirit lifted me up between earth and heaven and in visions of God he took me to Jerusalem, to the entrance to the north gate of the inner court, where the idol that provokes to jealousy stood. ...

Then he said to me, "Son of man, look toward the north." So I looked, and in the entrance north of the gate of the altar I saw this idol of jealousy. ...

Then he brought me to the entrance to the court. I looked, and I saw a hole in the wall. ...

So I went in and looked, and I saw portrayed all over the walls all kinds of crawling things and detestable animals and all the idols of the house of Israel. ...

He said to me, "Son of man, have you seen what the elders of the house of Israel are doing in the darkness, each at the shrine of his own idol? They say, 'The Lord does not see us; the Lord has forsaken the land.'" ...

Then he brought me to the entrance to the north gate of the house of the Lord, and I saw women sitting there, mourning for Tammuz.

- God's jealousy is an expression of His love.
- There is a difference between jealous *of* and jealous *for*. God is jealous *for* everything He created because it is His, it belongs to Him.
- If we could grasp the idea that God is jealous for us, our name, our lives, our hearts, and nothing else will substitute, it would change everything.
- If your deepest feelings are reserved for something besides God, then that is probably an idol that provokes God's jealousy.

Mark mentioned that God has feelings. How does that statement impact you? Is that something you've ever thought about before? When was the last time you were aware that your actions might have affected God's feelings?

SMALL-GROUP DIALOGUE—

God is jealous. He clearly states that rather unsettling fact throughout Scripture. What is it that provokes His jealousy? Anything that displaces God is an idol, and God opposes idols in our lives. There is evidence of that in Ezekiel 8.

EZEKIEL 8:1-5

In the sixth year, in the sixth month, on the fifth day of the month, I was sitting in my house and the elders of Judah were sitting in front of me, and there the hand of the Lord God came down on me. I looked, and there was a form that had the appearance of a man. From what seemed to be His waist down was fire, and from His waist up was something that looked bright, like the gleam of amber. He stretched out what appeared to be a hand and took me by the hair of my head. Then the Spirit lifted me up between earth and heaven and carried me in visions of God to Jerusalem, to the entrance of the inner gate that faces north, where the offensive statue that provokes jealousy was located. I saw the glory of the God of Israel there, like the vision I had seen in the plain. The Lord said to me, "Son of man, look toward the north." I looked to the north, and there was this offensive statue north of the altar gate, at the entrance.

Let's pause there. Most scholars believe that the idol reference here is the Canaanite goddess of fertility. It was their sex god. Sexual pleasure was their god. It was more important to them than God Himself. If you are like me, you read a story like this and wonder how people could be so silly as to whittle wood, call it a god, and then pray to it and worship it. It seems so foreign and ancient, doesn't it?

The reality is that we are simply more sophisticated sinners. Idolatry is still practiced today; we just don't make our idols out of wood.

In what ways do you think we are simply more sophisticated sinners?

Where do we find the equivalent of the Canaanite goddess of fertility in our culture today?

What other idols are prevalent in our culture today?

Let's continue reading in Ezekiel:

EZEKIEL 8:7-13

Then He brought me to the entrance of the court, and when I looked there was a hole in the wall. He said to me, "Son of man, dig through the wall." So I dug through the wall, and there was a doorway. He said to me, "Go in and see the terrible and detestable things they are committing here." I went in and looked, and there engraved all around the wall was every form of detestable thing, crawling creatures and beasts, as well as all the idols of the house of Israel. Seventy elders from the house of Israel were standing before them, with Jaazaniah son of Shaphan standing among them. Each had a firepan in his hand, and a fragrant cloud of incense was rising up. Then He said to me, "Son of man, do you see what the elders of the house of Israel are doing in the darkness, each at the shrine of his idol? For they are saying, 'The Lord does not see us. The Lord has abandoned the land.'" Again He said to me, "You will see even more detestable things, which they are committing."

All of us have hidden rooms where we practice secret sins or harbor sinful thoughts. For some of us, they are literal rooms like our bedroom, bathroom, or family room. For others, they are figurative rooms in our hearts and minds. When no one is looking, what are you doing in your hidden room? I think many of us have hidden rooms that are in essence idol factories.

Looking at Ezekiel 8:7-13, who were the people engaged in idolatrous practices in the hidden room?

When God points out a hidden room in our lives, what should be our response?

Do you think hidden rooms can be completely abolished in our lives or do we just have to lock the door, ignore them, and never go in again? Explain.

Let's keep reading…

EZEKIEL 8:14-15

So He brought me to the entrance of the north gate of the LORD's house, and I saw women sitting there weeping for Tammuz. And He said to me, "Do you see this, son of man? You will see even more detestable things than these."

Here, we discover yet another idol, Tammuz, the Babylonian goddess of spring. Instead of worshiping the God who created everything, they decided to give credit to and mourn an idol.

We must steward our emotions. There are moments we need to mourn because we have offended a jealous God. But sometimes we mourn for things less than worthy. We allow our day to be ruined by a person or conversation or action that we have esteemed higher than God's opinion. When that happens, we may have stumbled on a personal idol.

What things do you mourn or get upset over? What ruins your day?

If our hearts broke for the things that break the heart of God, what would we be mourning?

The vision continues…

EZEKIEL 8:16-18

So He brought me to the inner court of the Lord's house, and there were about 25 men at the entrance of the Lord's temple, between the portico and the altar, with their backs to the Lord's temple and their faces turned to the east. They were bowing to the east in worship of the sun. And He said to me, "Do you see this, son of man? Is it not enough for the house of Judah to commit the detestable things they are practicing here, that they must also fill the land with violence and repeatedly provoke Me to anger, even putting the branch to their nose? Therefore I will respond with wrath. I will not show pity or spare them. Though they cry out in My ears with a loud voice, I will not listen to them."

They bowed to the wrong god. They turned their backs on God and faced the wrong direction. In *The Weight of Glory*, C.S. Lewis says, "Our Lord finds our desires not too strong, but too weak. We are half-hearted creatures, fooling about with drink and sex and ambition when infinite joy is offered us, like an ignorant child who wants to go on making mud pies in a slum because he cannot imagine what is meant by the offer of a holiday at the sea. We are far too easily pleased."[1]

Describe a moment when you settled for less than God's blessing because you were "far too easily pleased."

What are some practical actions we can take and disciplines we can employ to strive for and wait with joyful anticipation for the infinite jealousy of Christ?

1. C.S. Lewis, *The Weight of Glory* (New York: HarperCollins Publishers, 1980), 26

WRAP ————————————————

God is jealous for us, and that jealousy is an expression of His love. He is jealous for the glory that is due Him, and He is jealous for the affection of those He created. Only God is worthy of our worship; everything else is at best a distraction and at worst an idol.

REMEMBER THESE KEY THOUGHTS FROM THIS WEEK'S STUDY:

- God is not jealous *of* anything. He is jealous *for* something.
- Jealousy is an expression of God's love.
- Anything that we reverence or worship above God is an idol.
- All of us have hidden rooms in our lives, hearts, and minds that we must allow the Holy Spirit to enter and redeem.

Over the course of the next week, begin each day proclaiming that the Lord is God and devote yourself to loving Him with all your heart, soul, and strength.

Next week we will explore the blissful perplexity of the sovereignty of God.

PURSUING GOD

There are places in Scripture that make me uncomfortable. There are verses that describe God differently than the way I like to think of Him. Like Nahum 1:2, "The Lord is a jealous and avenging God." I don't like to think of God as jealous. It makes Him seem … less God-like. But that word is specifically used at least 20 times in Scripture to describe the character of God, so we can't ignore it. When we hear the word *jealous*, we often equate that emotion with a moral flaw. Or confuse it with envy. When I come to verses that I want to skip over or that I wish were not included in the Bible, that's when I really need to slow down and dig deeper. If I read something about God's character or actions that doesn't seem to match up with the image of God I created in my head, then I must stop to make sure I'm not worshiping a false image of God, an image of my own making.

Maybe we should stop trying to fit God's character into our understanding of jealousy and instead look at jealousy in light of God's character. Envy is wanting what doesn't belong to you. Jealousy is protecting what is rightfully yours. God is never described as envious, but Scripture repeatedly confirms that He is jealous for His glory and jealous for His people.

Think about the difference between envy and jealousy. Identify a time you expressed envy and a time you expressed pure jealousy.

The jealousy of God rages and it burns against sin. It rails against idolatry. But God's jealousy for His glory and His people took Him to the cross, to the death of Jesus. His jealousy meant He had to pour out His wrath on His son on the cross.

So, if we are tempted to view God as being little because of His jealousy, we must remember where that jealousy led Him. If we view jealousy as unGodlike or are tempted to view it as a fallen, immoral response, then we must look on the blood-soaked cross where that jealousy manifested itself.

He stepped into the mess of our lives and bought back what rightfully belonged to Him. God is jealous for His name and for His people, and that jealousy drove Him to the cross. And it should drive us to our knees in worship.

PURSUING GOD

GOMER

The story of Hosea and Gomer might be the closest thing to jealous love we know outside the cross. God instructs Hosea to "take to yourself a wife of whoredom and have children of whoredom" (Hosea 1:2, ESV). Can you imagine? What would you do if your spouse (or future spouse) became a prostitute? Gomer is enslaved and actually prefers false love to the love of her husband. Devastating doesn't even begin to hint at how that must feel for Hosea. Scripture says, "She did not know that it was I who gave her the grain, the wine, and the oil, and who lavished on her silver and gold, which they used for Baal" (2:8, ESV).

The kind of love God called Hosea to show Gomer was not the love of natural affection. It was a love of the will, the stuff that covenants are made of. It's the choice to be loving and faithful even if your spouse is unlovable and unfaithful in return.

In the midst of Gomer's unfaithfulness, God calls to Hosea again, "Go again, love a woman who is loved by another man and is an adulteress" (3:1, ESV) and Hosea replies, "So I bought her for fifteen shekels of silver and a homer and a lethech of barley" (3:2, ESV).

The same way Hosea shows love to Gomer, God shows love to us. It is not Hosea we most identify with; it's Gomer. We are all Gomer, and God is so desirous of our affection and so deserving of our praise that He is willing to come to where we are, pay the going rate, and redeem us. God is that jealous.

Is there a moment in your life (a sin, conversation, decision, moment of weakness) that you are afraid may render you outside the scope of God's redemption? If so, how might Gomer's story change your thinking?

God turns our valleys of trouble to doors of hope. That's what the gospel is about. It's about the ways we run from God and the way He redeems us in the midst of our sin over and over again. Christ is our great Hosea.

PURSUING GOD

IDOL FACTORIES

Be careful not to make a treaty with those who live in the land where you are going, or
they will be a snare among you. Break down their altars, smash their sacred stones and
cut down their Asherah poles. Do not worship any other god, for the LORD, whose name
is Jealous, is a jealous God. (Exodus 34:12-14, NIV)

While idolatry sounds like an ancient pagan construct that has no bearing or relevance to our lives today, let's take a moment to consider what an idol is. An idol is anything that takes the place that rightfully belongs to God. It is anything we worship apart from Him.

We were created to worship. Whether we call it that or not, we all worship something. Sometimes we even create things to worship. Bottom line is we are either worshiping God or an idol.

It doesn't actually take a lot of my brain power to identify the idols in my life. They usually surface when I consider a few questions. Take a moment now to ask yourself the questions below. Invite the Holy Spirit into the process, asking: "Search me, God, and know my heart; test me and know my concerns. See if there is any offensive way in me; lead me in the everlasting way" (Psalm 139:23-24).

What demands my focus and affections?

From what do I derive my meaning? What or who do I look to to tell me who I am and what I'm worth?

Where do I find safety, refuge, comfort, pleasure, security, or shelter?

Who must I please? Whose opinion counts?

SESSION SIX

SOVEREIGNTY

Some of us want a democratic God, but that's not what we get. God is sovereign and His kingdom is just that—it is a kingdom with a King who is absolutely sovereign. And we have one option: complete submission of our lives to the lordship of Jesus Christ.

On one hand, it seems natural and easy to submit to His lordship. He loves us, cares for us, listens to us, and redeems us. We know that He is good, faithful, and merciful. Who wouldn't want to submit to that kind of king?

But how does God's sovereignty interact with man's free will? If God is sovereign, then why do bad things happen to good people? If God knows all and sees all, then why do we pray? When faced with these questions, we may find that it is more difficult to submit to His lordship and more natural to ask His actions to submit to our ideals of goodness and truth.

When we come to the end of every possible answer we can conceive, we are left with a choice. Do we believe that God is who He says He is? And do we believe that God is above everything and working through all things for our good and for His glory?

God is not offended or threatened by our questions about His sovereignty. The real question, however, is how we will respond when we recognize we will never have a perspective adequate enough to take into full account the bigness of God. So feel free to question. But recognize that ultimately, our response to God's sovereignty is not to question, but to worship.

Use this time to talk with your group about how God has revealed Himself to you since last week's study.

How do you think about jealousy and idolatry differently after last week's study?

After completing the study on jealousy, what idols did you notice in our culture?

Do you think that God cares and governs over the smallest and most minute details in the universe? Is there anything He does not care about? Explain.

Does God's sovereignty interact or clash with the free will of mankind? Why?

Fill in the blanks below on important points as you view the message from Mark. You'll unpack this information with the group after the video.

Sometimes God shows _____. Sometimes God shows _____.

There is a heavenly Father who cares about every

_____ _____ of His creation.

When there are questions we cannot answer, it is very important that we zoom out

and get some _____.

We falsely accuse and find fault in _____ because we are totally

oblivious to the fact that we were born on a battlefield, that there is a very

real Enemy who wants to _____, _____,

and _____.

MATTHEW 10:29-31, NIV

Are not two sparrows sold for a penny? Yet not one of them will fall to the ground apart from the will of your Father. And even the very hairs of your head are all numbered. So don't be afraid; you are worth more than many sparrows.

PROVERBS 16:9, NIV

In his heart a man plans his course, but the LORD determines his steps.

JOHN 10:10

A thief comes only to steal and to kill and to destroy. I have come so that they may have life and have it in abundance.

- God is great not only because nothing is too big for Him, but also because nothing is too small for Him. He cares about every detail.

- Maybe sometimes we don't see who God is or don't understand His sovereignty because we get up so close that we can't see the entire painting.

- Until we believe in the existence of a very real, very active Enemy, we will make the mistake of blaming the bad things that happen on God instead of on Satan.

- C.S. Lewis said that God cast His vote for us when Christ died at Calvary. Satan cast his vote against us. And we cast the deciding vote.

Mark asks the question: "If God is omnipotent and omniscient, all-powerful and all-knowing, and there is nothing not subject to His authority, if God is sovereign, then why do bad things happen?" How do you respond to that question?

SMALL-GROUP DIALOGUE—

God is great not only because nothing is too big for Him, but also because nothing is too small for Him. Jesus described it this way:

MATTHEW 10:29-31

Aren't two sparrows sold for a penny? Yet not one of them falls to the ground without your Father's consent. But even the hairs of your head have all been counted. So don't be afraid therefore; you are worth more than many sparrows.

Because we don't live in a first-century Jewish culture, we may fail to grasp the full power of this passage. A sparrow was the cheapest ticket item in the food market in that day and age. You could purchase two of them for one of the smallest and least valuable coins. Jesus is telling us that we have a heavenly Father who cares about every minute detail of His creation. How much more does He care about you and me?

What are some of the small details of your life that you are currently concerned about?

With the recognition that God cares about those details, how can you practically involve God in your thoughts, conversations, and actions related to those details?

We often fail to express our gratitude to God for His sustaining presence in our lives because we don't stop to recognize how intimately He is involved. For instance, when was the last time you thanked God that the sun appeared this morning? Or that you continued to breathe through the night?

Because God is concerned about details that may escape our notice, take a moment to consider how He is active in your life. Write down 2-3 ways that you can be more aware of and thankful for His involvement in your life.

One area where we tend to question the sovereignty of God is when it relates to His will for our individual lives. In some moments, we desperately want to know that God is in charge and has a wonderful plan for us, and we will invest hours of prayer into discovering what that is. Other times we aren't sure what we think about God's sovereignty in our lives. We are glad that God loves us, but we don't know how interested we are in that wonderful plan He has for our lives. After all, we have pretty good plans for ourselves.

The writer of Proverbs addresses this tension between our free will and God's sovereignty.

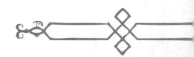

PROVERBS 16:9

A man's heart plans his way, but the LORD determines his steps.

What does this passage tell us about the tension between the sovereignty of God and the free will of man?

When the sovereignty of God clashes with the free will of man, which one wins?

Here's the problem with the sovereignty of God: children who can't swim fall into pools and drown. Innocent people are hit by drunk drivers. Children who can't defend themselves are abused. And there are tens of thousands who will die of starvation today because they can't find any food to eat. My question is this—how do you juxtapose that with Scripture? I don't think it takes away from those sovereign moments where God's invisible hand is clearly evident, but I also don't think we can ignore the pain and suffering and tragedy that happens in this life.

Why doesn't God keep the sparrow from falling? Why doesn't He keep the child from drowning? Why doesn't He cure all cancer and stop all accidents or end all starvation? If He is omnipotent, and the word *sovereign* means all-powerful and all-knowing and that there is nothing not subject to His authority, then why do bad things happen? I think that's where many of us get stuck spiritually. Why doesn't an all-powerful, all-knowing, ever-present God step in and save the day?

Ultimately we must embrace the idea that God's sovereignty and our free will work together in supernatural tension and cooperation to bring about His purposes for our good and His glory.

How do you respond to moments in life when you feel that your free will might conflict with God's sovereignty?

We live in a fallen world where bad situations are going to happen. God often responds in one of three ways. There are certainly countless times when He prevents bad things from happening to us. Other times, He intervenes in the moment and rescues us from, protects us from, and overturns adversity. Sometimes, His response is redemption— stepping in after those bad things happen and using them for our good and His glory.

Identify a time when God's response to a bad circumstance in your life was intervention and a time when His response was redemption.

As believers we can rest and find peace in the knowledge that God redeems all things—some in this world but all in the life to come. Sometimes God's sovereignty presents us with challenging questions we will never be able to answer this side of eternity. In session 1 I talked about my Deuteronomy 29:29 file. The question is not, Will bad things happen? The question is, How will we respond when the real or perceived actions of God (or perhaps more commonly, inactions of God) don't line up with what we believe about His character and goodness?

At the end of the day, we may have to decide whether we are going to question God's sovereignty or trust and celebrate it. I wonder if too often we put ourselves in the position where we demand that God prove Himself to us. Job faced this in his life. Was what Job went through fair? No! But I think the longer I live, the more I realize that you can't determine the cards in your hand. You are dealt a hand and the only thing you can do is decide how you are going to play that hand. You have to deal with the dealer and make a decision—am I going to question God or am I going to submit to His sovereignty?

Job went head-to-head with God over the challenges that God allowed in his life and he presented God with some hard questions. God responded to Job with some questions of His own in chapters 38–40. When I need to recalibrate my perspective, I read these verses:

JOB 38:3-4,12,24,31-35

Get ready to answer Me like a man;

when I question you, you will inform Me.

Where were you when I established the earth?

Tell Me, if you have understanding. ...

Have you ever in your life commanded the morning

or assigned the dawn its place? ...

What road leads to the place where light is dispersed?

Where is the source of the east wind that spreads across the earth? ...

Can you fasten the chains of the Pleiades

or loosen the belt of Orion?

Can you bring out the constellations in their season

and lead the Bear and her cubs?

Do you know the laws of heaven?

Can you impose its authority on earth?

Can you command the clouds

so that a flood of water covers you?

Can you send out lightning bolts, and they go?

Do they report to you: "Here we are"?

How does God's response to Job challenge your understanding of His character?

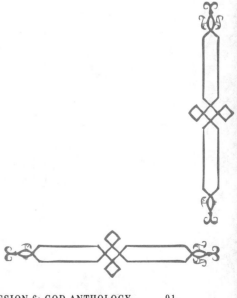

WRAP

God is all-knowing, ever-present, and full of divine power. While His sovereignty is not something we can always understand or explain, it ensures that His purposes will be fulfilled for our good and for His glory.

REMEMBER THESE KEY THOUGHTS FROM THIS WEEK'S STUDY:

- The kingdom of God is not a democracy. It is a kingdom with a good King.
- God is great not only because nothing is too big for Him, but also because nothing is too small for Him.
- In God's story, His sovereignty and our free will work together in supernatural tension and cooperation to fulfill His purposes.
- When we come to the end of our understanding, we can either question God's sovereignty or we can celebrate it.

In addition to the attributes we have mentioned in this study, write down five characteristics that you associate with God:

-
-
-
-
-

As you read the Scriptures, consider highlighting every place you see a name or attribute of God. His character will jump off of the pages. Pray that as you see God more clearly, you can worship Him more rightly and look more like Him.

PURSUING GOD

When we think about the control panel of our lives, one of the most basic and primary lessons a Christ-follower will face is the question of who is in charge. Let's be real: we are all a bit control-freakish. *Who's in charge here?* is a question we wrestle with, and for the sake of our souls we must ask it again and again.

What circumstances in your life are you trying to control right now? Take a moment and write a short prayer inviting God to take control of those circumstances in your life.

The philosophy behind the Enlightenment argued that human reason is the most superior form of authority. Also called The Age of Reason, the Enlightenment taught that we could advance humanity and create a better world through intellectual and scientific gain. An inevitable result of the Enlightenment was a culture of hyper-focus on the self, resulting in a sense of confusion over ultimate identity and ultimate authority. This marked a shift of man's attention from divine authority onto himself.

The church is not exempt. When we read the Bible, we often read it through a "me" filter. *How does this apply to me? What's this got to do with me?* That's like going to a movie to see the extras, those insignificant characters who are hired to be fillers. Likewise, the Bible is first and foremost the story of God, not us.

The message is quite simple. God is the Creator who is reconciling all things, including you and me, to Himself. He's done this through the Person and work of Jesus Christ. It was His plan and promise in the Old Testament and the mystery revealed in the New Testament. And we do have a role. He brings us—you and me individually, as well as us together as His church—into His plan.

When we read the Bible for all its worth and have a right understanding of Who it is about, we find that we are not all that unimportant. We have a place in God's story; we are sons and daughters of the King. When we submit to our true Authority, we find our true identity.

PURSUING GOD

How many times have we hijacked the story of God and fashioned it into a weapon to wield for our own purposes? We've turned it into a history book, a science textbook, a systematic theology, a political platform. We've turned it into a story about us. But it's ultimately not about us. It's the story of a passionate God on a relentless pursuit to rescue His creation lost to the ugliness of sin. It's the story of the salvation of the entire creation found inside a gigantic boat. The tale of shepherd boys slaying giants and slaves promoted to prime ministers and Jewish orphans crowned as queens of Persia. It's the story of a God coming wrapped in the skin of His own creation and subjecting Himself to the care of fallen humanity.

Jesus once said, "I will build My church, and the forces of Hades will not overpower it" (Matthew 16:18). Not only that, but the folly of man will not overcome it. Nor the pride or insecurity of those who will lead the church. The heresies and hypocrisies of those who claim to stand for the truth cannot undermine the divine purposes and plans of God. Persecutions cannot overcome it. Inquisitions cannot overcome it. Crusades cannot overcome it.

Describe a moment in your own life when God's sovereignty prevailed in spite of your weakness, bad decisions, or sin.

When we talk of sovereignty, we often get hung up on intricate details of how much control God has over every situation, decision, and consequence that we face. But when viewed from a more eternal perspective, it would be foolish and irrational to argue that He is anything less than completely sovereign. This is His story. He is writing it, and it is ultimately about Him.

PURSUING GOD

We know that all things work together for the good of those who love God: those who are called according to His purpose. (Romans 8:28)

God is sovereign and He is mindful. Remember the story of Jacob and Leah? She was Jacob's first wife, though he never meant to marry her. His eye had been captured by Leah's younger sister Rachel. The Bible tells it all—there was no sparkle in Leah's eyes, but Rachel was beautiful. Jacob meant to marry Rachel, but he woke up to Leah. Jacob's life was not the only one ruined on that day; Leah's story would be marked with insecurity, rejection, jealousy, manipulation, and pain. Yet God was mindful of her.

Write down 2-3 other stories in Scripture where God noticed someone who was overlooked or shoved to the fringes of society. For each one, what do you learn about the character of God?

Leah named her first three children Reuben ("The Lord noticed my misery."), Simeon ("The Lord knows I am unloved."), and Levi ("My husband will surely feel affection for me."). She named her fourth child Judah, which means "Now I will praise the Lord." (See Genesis 29:32-35.)

In Judah, Leah finally gets a glimpse that the Lord is bigger than her situation and had taken notice of her. She learns to praise God despite her circumstances.

Fast forward the story of God, and we find that it is out of the tribe of Judah that Jesus was born. He's the Good Shepherd who will leave His flock and come after you and me when we are lost. He knows us by name, and He teaches us His voice. He is the One who was before the world began and is sovereign over the events of our lives and the choices we make. Secretly and not so secretly working, weaving all things together for good because we are called according to His purpose.

The story of God is for Leah, for you, and for me.

LEADER GUIDE ─────────────

HOW TO USE THIS STUDY

We're glad you've chosen to take your small group through *The God Anthology*. It is our prayer that this study will guide your group into a right understanding of God—stripping away the false picture we have painted and restoring a proper vista of who God is based on what He has revealed in Scripture. Before you get started, here is some helpful information about the different elements you'll encounter within the study as well as the resources you will find on the following pages.

WEEK INTRODUCTION

Each session begins with an overview of the weekly topic. This material is designed to help you introduce the aspect of God's character to be discussed each week. You will probably want to read this before your group meets so that you'll better understand the topic and the context for your time together. For weeks 2-6, suggest that group members also read this before you meet.

IN RETROSPECT

This time is designed to provide group members with an opportunity to talk about what God has been revealing to them or what internal dialogue or conclusions have resulted from their personal time during the past week.

FRAMING THE STORY

Your actual group time will most likely begin here with an icebreaker that is designed to help you ease into the study and get everyone talking. These questions are intended to be nonthreatening to group members so that a pattern of participation can be established early on.

VIDEO DISCUSSION

The first page of this section provides group members with a listening guide they can use to fill in the blanks on important points as they view Mark's video message.

The second page is designed as follow-up to the video message. The bulleted items highlight the main teaching points from the video and can be used to process within the group what they heard and how they were affected. The discussion question directly relates to the video message and allows group members an opportunity for more personal application.

SMALL-GROUP DIALOGUE

This portion of your weekly group meeting will guide group members to study passages that reinforce what Mark teaches in his video message. Each question is designed to lead the group deeper into the truth of the Scriptures they are studying and give them an opportunity to integrate these truths into their own lives.

WRAP

This section serves as a conclusion to the group time and summarizes key points from your small-group meeting each week.

PURSUING GOD

These three pages following each small-group session are intended to give group members an opportunity to take what they've learned during the session and continue the conversation in private devotional settings with God.

Another item we've included on the following pages is a copy of the video listening guides for each session with answers. These may be useful to you if someone misses a session and would like to fill in the blanks.

In addition to the general notes to help you along the way, we have taken each question from the small-group discussion time and provided an explanation for why it is included as well as examples of possible responses when applicable. You will find this information on the DVD-ROM in your leader kit. We hope the information we have provided will better equip you to lead your study each week.

The God Anthology music CD in your leader kit can be utilized to enhance your small-group experience in any way you wish. You can also find additional resources on *godanthology.com* such as song lyrics, chord charts, and behind-the-scenes videos.

LEADER GUIDE ——————
SESSION ONE

MYSTERY

WEEK INTRODUCTION

Welcome group members to *The God Anthology* study and make sure everyone has a member book. You may want to consider jumping to the In Retrospect session first this week and then come back to the narrative overview on page 7 to help you introduce the topic of study for session 1.

IN RETROSPECT

In weeks 2-6 this time will be used to talk about what God has been revealing to group members or what conclusions or internal dialogue have resulted from their devotion time during the week. In this session, however, you'll talk in more broad terms as group members consider which characteristics they most associate with God as well as which characteristics are most confusing, frightening, or unsettling.

FRAMING THE STORY

Since this is the first week of your small-group study, it might be a good idea to spend some time getting to know one another. The questions in this section will help facilitate that. Therefore, it is recommended that you have everyone in the group respond to all of the questions. Even if you have been walking together as a group for a while, this study will reveal new things about everyone's personalities, hopes, dreams, and fears; and the subject matter lends itself to talking in depth about our character. Some members of your group will be more comfortable speaking aloud than others. Remember that the objective is to get everyone involved.

VIDEO DISCUSSION

Play the video titled "Mystery" (16:00). Encourage group members to follow along, fill in the blanks on page 10, and take additional notes as they hear things that speak strongly to their own stories.

————————————————————————

Our biggest problem is our <u>small</u> <u>view</u> <u>of</u> <u>God</u>.

The goal isn't just to know more information. The goal is <u>transformation</u>.

One of our most dangerous tendencies is to <u>deify</u> man and <u>humanize</u> God.

If you lose the mystery, it is called <u>idolatry.</u>

Humility in the presence of mystery is called <u>the fear of God.</u>

We offer answers; God offers a <u>relationship</u> through Jesus Christ.

After the group has viewed the video, direct their attention to page 11. Read through the Scripture passages at the top of the page as well as the main points from the video message that are bulleted below. You may choose to do this yourself or ask volunteers from the group to read portions aloud. This time is intended for discussion within the group about what they heard, how they were affected, and personal application. As time permits, allow group members to share other thoughts they had from the video.

SMALL-GROUP DIALOGUE

In session 1 you will look as a group at 1 Corinthians 2:1-10, Deuteronomy 29:29, and Romans 16:25-27 to explore the mysterious nature of God and to consider how that attribute of God's personality can leave us both amazed and confused.

Check the DVD-ROM in your leader kit for possible answers to the group questions. You might also want to play the song "Mystery" from *The God Anthology* worship CD as you close out your study time. Encourage group members to use this time to reflect on what God has shown them about Himself through this week's study and how they can use what they've learned to become more like Him.

WRAP

At this point each week, you will want to close the group time in prayer. For this week, it's probably best for you to pray for the group. In coming weeks, as group members get more comfortable, consider asking for volunteers to lead the group in prayer.

PURSUING GOD

Encourage group members to complete these pages before your next group meeting and remind them that you will be discussing what God has shown them through their time with Him. Also remind them to read the introduction to session 2 before they come.

Share that next week you'll explore the holiness of God—God is not simply some bigger, better version of us; He is wholly good and wholly other. He is in a category entirely to Himself.

LEADER GUIDE ——————
SESSION TWO

HOLINESS

WEEK INTRODUCTION

Welcome group members back. Use the narrative overview on page 21 to help you introduce the topic of study for session 2. Make sure you read this before your group meets so that you'll better understand the topic and the context for your time together.

IN RETROSPECT

The questions in this section allow group members to share some of their devotional reflections and life applications to the previous week's topic. This week you will be talking about what God has been revealing to group members regarding the mystery of God and how God does extraordinary things in the midst of the ordinary.

FRAMING THE STORY

Give everyone an opportunity to answer the first question. Then do the same for the second and third. Or, if time is a factor, choose one or two questions that you feel would be the most appropriate for the group and ask everyone to answer those. Continue to encourage all group members to share during this time.

VIDEO DISCUSSION

Play the video titled "Holiness" (17:00). Encourage group members to follow along, fill in the blanks on page 24, and take additional notes as they hear things that speak strongly to their own stories.

————————————————————

Your outlook on life is determined by your internal representation of who God is.

The word *holy* means absolutely good. The word *holy* means wholly means wholly other.

A.W. Tozer said God's holiness is not simply the best we know infinitely bettered, it is unapproachable, unattainable, incomprehensible.

Without the woe of God, you cannot enter into the wow of God.

We underestimate the mercy of God because we underestimate the holiness of God.

You won't see God seated on the throne if you're <u>standing</u>.

It's not until we completely submit our lives to the <u>lordship</u> of Jesus Christ that we have a revelation of His holiness.

_____

After the group has viewed the video, direct their attention to page 25. Read through the Scripture passages at the top of the page as well as the main points from the video message that are bulleted below. You may choose to do this yourself or ask volunteers from the group to read portions aloud. This time is intended for discussion within the group about what they heard, how they were affected, and personal application. As time permits, allow group members to share other thoughts they had from the video.

SMALL-GROUP DIALOGUE

In session 2 you will explore in depth Isaiah's encounter with God, how that affected him spiritually, emotionally, and physically, and how it prepared him to be established as one of God's leading prophetic voices to the nation of Israel. Using Isaiah 6:1-8 as a guide, you will discuss spiritual disciplines such as worship and confession and attitudes like humility and submission. You will also explore the connection and tension between posturing yourself before God and positioning yourself before men.

Check the DVD-ROM in your leader kit for possible answers to the group questions. You might also want to play the song "All Things" from *The God Anthology* worship CD as you close out your study time. Encourage group members to use this time to reflect on what God has shown them about Himself through this week's study and how they can use what they've learned to become more like Him.

WRAP

Close the group in a time of prayer. This week you may consider asking for a volunteer to lead the group. Use the Lord's Prayer as a way to close out the group time. It is printed for you on page 32.

PURSUING GOD

Remind and encourage group members to complete these pages before your next group meeting. Also remind them to read the introduction to session 3 before they come. Share that next week you'll explore the incomparable nature of God—God is incomparably wise, gracious, loving, and powerful. There is absolutely no comparison between God and us. He is not a little bit bigger, a little bit better, a little bit stronger, a little bit wiser; He is so much more than that.

LEADER GUIDE ———————
SESSION THREE

INCOMPARABILITY

WEEK INTRODUCTION

Welcome group members back. Use the narrative overview on page 37 to help you introduce the topic of study for session 3. Make sure you read this before your group meets so that you'll better understand the topic and the context for your time together.

IN RETROSPECT

The questions in this section allow group members to share some of the practical implications of last week's study on the holiness of God. This week you will be talking about the ways group members engaged worship differently over the past week as well as how their view of God's holiness is practically impacting their lives on a daily basis.

FRAMING THE STORY

Give everyone an opportunity to answer the first question. Then do the same for the second. Group members should be getting more comfortable with sharing by this point in your study.

VIDEO DISCUSSION

Play the video titled "Incomparability" (10:00). Encourage group members to follow along, fill in the blanks on page 40, and take additional notes as they hear things that speak strongly to their own stories.

————————————————————

God's power is not just incomparable. His power isn't just great. His power is <u>incomparably</u> <u>great</u>.

In order to comprehend God's incomparable love, grace, and power, we need <u>revelation</u>. We need to get into His <u>Word</u> and into His <u>presence</u> and ask Him to reveal it to us.

While God's power is measureless, the prophet Isaiah gives us a glimpse of His omnipotence by comparing it to the size of the <u>universe.</u>

Even the most brilliant among us underestimate God by <u>15.5 billion</u> <u>light</u> <u>years</u>.

————————————————————

After the group has viewed the video, direct their attention to page 41. Read through the Scripture passages at the top of the page as well as the main points from the video message that are bulleted below. You may choose to do this yourself or ask volunteers from the group to read portions aloud. This time is intended for discussion within the group about what they heard, how they were affected, and personal application. As time permits, allow group members to share other thoughts they had from the video.

SMALL-GROUP DIALOGUE

In session 3 you will use Paul's prayer for the church in Ephesus in Ephesians 1:16-23 to explore our small view of God and our perception of how big He really is. Encourage group members to recognize that God is bigger than their biggest problems but also aware of the smallest details of their lives.

Check the DVD-ROM in your leader kit for possible answers to the group questions.

WRAP

Close the group time in prayer or ask for a volunteer to lead the group. A prayer from A.W. Tozer's *Knowledge of the Holy* has been included on page 46 for your use if you desire.

PURSUING GOD

Remind and encourage group members to complete these pages before your next group meeting. Also remind them to read the introduction to session 4 before they come. Share that next week you'll explore the mercy of God.

LEADER GUIDE ———————
SESSION FOUR

MERCY

WEEK INTRODUCTION

Welcome group members back. Use the narrative overview on page 51 to help you introduce the topic of study for session 4. Make sure you read this before your group meets so that you'll better understand the topic and the context for your time together.

IN RETROSPECT

This week you'll be talking about how group members' image of God is changing over the course of this study as well as what big, impossible prayers they are praying.

FRAMING THE STORY

Give everyone an opportunity to answer the first question. Then do the same for the second. Continue to encourage all group members to share during this time.

VIDEO DISCUSSION

Play the video titled "Mercy" (13:00). Encourage group members to follow along, fill in the blanks on page 54, and take additional notes as they hear things that speak strongly to their own stories.

———————————————————

Mercy is like a <u>hammock,</u> where you rest all of your body weight in the wonderful <u>grace</u> of God.

The word *Lord* translated in the Old Testament is the name "Elohim" and it denotes the <u>mercy</u> of God. The word *God* is the Hebrew word "Jehovah" which denotes His <u>justice</u>.

<u>Repentance</u> activates the mercy of God.

Mercy is God <u>holding</u> <u>back</u> what we deserve and *grace* is God <u>giving</u> us what we don't deserve.

We can approach the throne of grace with <u>confidence</u>.

———————————————————

After the group has viewed the video, direct their attention to page 55. Read through the Scripture passages at the top of the page as well as the main points from the video message that are bulleted below. You may choose to do this yourself or ask volunteers from the group to read portions aloud. This time is intended for discussion within the group about what they heard, how they were affected, and personal application. As time permits, allow group members to share other thoughts they had from the video.

SMALL-GROUP DIALOGUE

In session 4 you will talk about Jesus' response to the woman caught in the act of adultery (John 8:3-11) and how we stand before Christ's mercy ourselves. Micah 6:6-8 brings the discussion to how we reflect the character of Christ in the ways we interact with those around us. Questions revolve around the relationship between justice, mercy, and humility and how we can practically show mercy in the world around us. Finally, the discussion moves to Hebrews 4:14-16 to reflect on the relationship between grace and mercy and the importance of confession.

Check the DVD-ROM in your leader kit for possible answers to the group questions. You might also want to play the song "Show Your Mercy" from *The God Anthology* worship CD as you close out your study time. Encourage group members to use this time to reflect on what God has shown them about Himself through this week's study and how they can use what they've learned to become more like Him.

WRAP

Open the floor for anyone to pray who feels led, and ask for a volunteer to close your time in prayer.

PURSUING GOD

Remind and encourage group members to complete these pages before your next group meeting. Also remind them to read the introduction to session 5 before they come. Share that next week you'll explore the jealousy of God and what that really means.

LEADER GUIDE ———————
SESSION FIVE

JEALOUSY

WEEK INTRODUCTION

Welcome group members back. Use the narrative overview on page 65 to help you introduce the topic of study for session 5. Make sure you read this before your group meets so that you'll better understand the topic and the context for your time together.

IN RETROSPECT

This week you'll be talking as a group about how last week's study on mercy affects the way group members look at and relate to other people as well as how they responded to the devotional activity: Imagine that you headed into a situation in which you expected to be a slave only to learn that you are being adopted.

FRAMING THE STORY

Give everyone an opportunity to answer the first question. Then do the same for the second. Continue to encourage all group members to share during this time. There could be a wide range of responses to these questions depending on how members understand the idea of jealousy. Encourage group members to base their responses in Scripture and what they know of the other attributes of God

VIDEO DISCUSSION

Play the video titled "Jealousy" (13:00). Encourage group members to follow along, fill in the blanks on page 68, and take additional notes as they hear things that speak strongly to their own stories.

————————————————————

We don't appreciate the <u>jealousy</u> of God because we don't understand the <u>love</u> of God.

God is not jealous <u>of</u> anything. But He is jealous <u>for</u> you.

What provokes God's jealousy? Anything that diverts our <u>attention</u> or our <u>affection</u> to someone or something else.

If you want to know if something is an idol, gauge your <u>feelings</u>.

If Jesus is not Lord <u>of</u> all, He is not Lord <u>at</u> all.

————————————————————

After the group has viewed the video, direct their attention to page 69. Read through the Scripture passages at the top of the page as well as the main points from the video message that are bulleted below. You may choose to do this yourself or ask volunteers from the group to read portions aloud. This time is intended for discussion within the group about what they heard, how they were affected, and personal application. As time permits, allow group members to share other thoughts they had from the video.

SMALL-GROUP DIALOGUE

In session 5 you will look in depth at a book that is likely rarely studied by most group members. Through Ezekiel 8, they will see how we are exposed to several kinds of idols and will be challenged to consider how those idols manifest themselves in our culture today. The outcome of group discussion should lead to the awareness that God's jealousy is rooted in His goodness and is leveraged for our highest good. God is not jealous of anything; He is jealous for His glory and for us.

Check the DVD-ROM in your leader kit for possible answers to the group questions. You might also want to play the song "Jealous God" from *The God Anthology* worship CD as you close out your study time. Encourage group members to use this time to reflect on what God has shown them about Himself through this week's study and how they can use what they've learned to become more like Him.

WRAP

Ask a volunteer in the group to close with a time of prayer.

PURSUING GOD

Remind and encourage group members to complete these pages before your next group meeting. Also remind them to read the introduction to session 6 before they come. Share that next week you'll explore how God is above everything and working through all things for your good and for His glory.

You'll also want to begin talking about what is next for your group when you complete your study of *The God Anthology*.

LEADER GUIDE ——————
SESSION SIX

SOVEREIGNTY

WEEK INTRODUCTION

Welcome group members back. Use the narrative overview on page 81 to help you introduce the topic of study for session 6. Make sure you read this before your group meets so that you'll better understand the topic and the context for your time together.

IN RETROSPECT

The questions in this section allow group members to share how the study of God's jealousy affected their awareness of idolatry in their own lives and in the culture around them.

FRAMING THE STORY

Give everyone an opportunity to answer the first question. Then do the same for the second. Be prepared for differences of opinion and tension in responses. Encourage group members to base their responses in Scripture and what they know of the other attributes of God. Help the group recognize that they feel this tension, at least in part, because God's mysterious, holy, incomparable nature renders Him not fully understandable by us. We can't put Him in a nice, neat, logical box. And that's OK. It should lead us to greater expressions of worship.

VIDEO DISCUSSION

Play the video titled "Sovereignty" (12:00). Encourage group members to follow along, fill in the blanks on page 84, and take additional notes as they hear things that speak strongly to their own stories.

———————————————————

Sometimes God shows <u>up.</u> Sometimes God shows <u>off.</u>

There is a heavenly Father who cares about every <u>minute</u> <u>detail</u> of His creation.

When there are questions we cannot answer, it is very important that we zoom out and get some <u>perspective</u>.

We falsely accuse and find fault in <u>God</u> because we are totally oblivious to the fact that we were born on a battlefield, that there is a very real Enemy who wants to <u>steal, kill,</u> and <u>destroy</u>.

———————————————————

After the group has viewed the video, direct their attention to page 85. Read through the Scripture passages at the top of the page as well as the main points from the video message that are bulleted below. You may choose to do this yourself or ask volunteers from the group to read portions aloud. This time is intended for discussion within the group about what they heard, how they were affected, and personal application. As time permits, allow group members to share other thoughts they had from the video.

SMALL-GROUP DIALOGUE

Through a study of Matthew 10:29-31 you will examine the level of detail in which God pays attention to your life. Proverbs 16:9 will guide discussion around the tension between God's sovereignty and man's free will. A series of passages from Job provide a reality check that we can never fully comprehend all that God is.

Check the DVD-ROM in your leader kit for possible answers to the group questions. You might also want to play the song "In Your Sovereignty" from *The God Anthology* worship CD as you close out your study time. Encourage group members to use this time to reflect on what God has shown them about Himself through this week's study and how they can use what they've learned to become more like Him.

WRAP

Ask group members to pray together to wrap up *The God Anthology* study. Take a few moments to recognize God for who He is, praising Him for His attributes and character, and asking Him to form those same attributes in you.

PURSUING GOD

Your group won't have an opportunity to process what God has shown them through their time with Him this week, but go ahead and remind them of the importance of completing these pages anyway.